9-21-11

EDGE BOOKS™

THE KIDS' GUIDE TO PRO WRESTLING

By Sean Stewart Price

Consultant:
Mike Johnson
PWInsider.com

CAPSTONE PRESS
a capstone imprint

Edge Books are published by Capstone Press,
151 Good Counsel Drive, P.O. Box 669, Mankato, Minnesota 56002.
www.capstonepub.com

 Books published by Capstone Press are manufactured with paper
containing at least 10 percent post-consumer waste.

Library of Congress Cataloging-in-Publication Data
Price, Sean Stewart.
    The kids' guide to pro wrestling / by Sean Stewart Price.
    p. cm. — (Edge. Kids' guides)
    Includes bibliographical references and index.
    Summary: "Describes the ins and outs of professional wrestling, including history,
gimmicks, and famous wrestlers"—Provided by publisher.
    ISBN 978-1-4296-6008-2 (library binding)
    1. Wrestling—Juvenile literature. I. Title.
GV1195.3.P75 2012
796.812—dc22   2011002486

Editorial Credits
Mandy Robbins, editor; Juliette Peters, designer; Wanda Winch,
    media researcher; Eric Manske, production specialist

Photo Credits
Corbis: Bettmann, 10, Duomo, 24; Getty Images Inc.: Ethan Miller, 15, Mark
Dadswell, 17, Ollie Millington/Redferns, 18, Sports Illustrated/Robert Beck,
11, Sports Illustrated/Stephen Green-Armytage, 16, Time Life Pictures/Myron
Davis, 26, WireImage/Bob Levy, 9; Library of Congress: Prints and Photographs
Division, 6; Newscom: Greg Henkenhaf, 20, Icon SMI 118/CITYFILES/
Alexandre Pona, 23, imago sportfotodienst, 4, 27, Jim Sulley, 21, SIPA/John
Smock, 29, Zuma Press/i01, cover (top), 13, Zuma Press/Mary Ann Owen,
cover (bottom), Zuma Press/r72, 12, 14, 25; Photo by Wrealano@aol.com, 28;
Shutterstock: Alfgar, chain link fence design, Allgusak, orange design element,
Paul Bodea, 7, Pavel Vakhrushev, cover (fireworks), relishtheglamor, Tribal art
design element

Printed in the United States of America in Stevens Point, Wisconsin.

032011   006111WZF11

TABLE OF CONTENTS

WELCOME to the RING!

Two giant men prowl around the wrestling ring looking for a way to attack. Sweat covers their bodies. The cheers of the crowd are deafening. Suddenly, one of the men sees an opening. He charges!

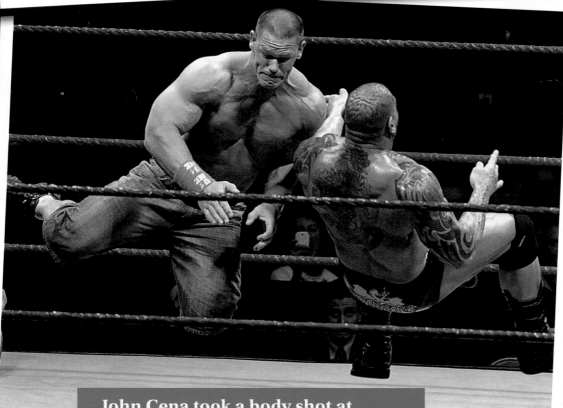

John Cena took a body shot at Batista during the main event of the Catch Revenge Tour in April 2010.

Pro wrestling matches are full of action. But long before the wrestling begins, wrestlers put on a show. Wrestlers make grand entrances as fans cheer. They parade around in flashy outfits. And they make grand speeches boasting of their amazing abilities.

In some ways, today's pro wrestlers are carrying on a tradition that is thousands of years old. Wrestling is one of the world's oldest sports. But wrestlers from ancient times might not recognize their sport in today's pro wrestling. Pro wrestling has become more about the show than any actual athletic contest. Yet pro wrestling is beloved by millions of people.

FUN FACT:

Pro wrestling is different from the wrestling that is done in high school, college, and the Olympics. Greco-Roman, freestyle, and folkstyle wrestling carry on the ancient traditions of wrestling.

A New Style of Wrestling

Professional wrestling began in the late 1800s. Carnival "strongmen" would challenge people to wrestle. The carnivals traveled the United States. They turned these matches into big shows that drew huge crowds. By the 1940s, these shows had become permanent in many big cities.

Carnival wrestling was a huge draw for spectators.

At first, professional wrestling was not as popular as other types of entertainment. That began to change with the invention of the TV. By the late 1940s, most American families owned a TV. In 1945 Los Angeles TV station KTLA broadcast the first pro wrestling match. It was an immediate hit. Soon all the big TV networks began airing wrestling shows.

Today most famous wrestlers work for the company World Wrestling Entertainment (WWE). Many others work for Total Nonstop Action Wrestling (TNA).

Heels and Babyfaces

Pro wrestling has two types of characters—bad guys and good guys. Bad guys are known as heels. Good guys are called babyfaces.

A heel actually wants the audience to boo him. He'll cheat, take cheap shots, or use dangerous **chokeholds**. Heels pick fights with babyfaces. They also often shout at fans, which is called "cheap heat." Cheap heat gets audiences booing the heel and cheering for the babyface.

A babyface receives both sympathy and respect from the fans. But he has to do so without appearing weak. Many wrestlers prefer being a heel to being a babyface. To them, it is easier and more fun to play the bad guy than to walk the fine line of a babyface.

chokehold—a hold that cuts off an opponent's breathing

FUN FACT:

The Miz is a well-known WWE heel. His catchphrase is, "I'm the Miz, and I'm awesome!"

What does it take to be a great heel or babyface? Two of wrestling's greatest characters will show you how it's done.

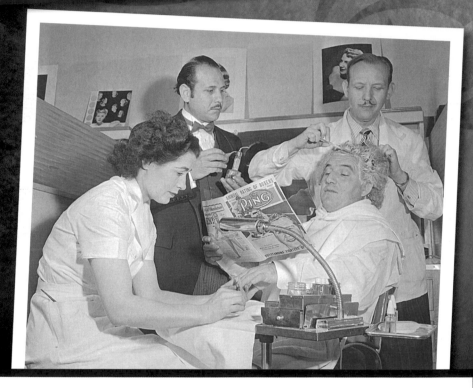

Gorgeous George

George Wagner did not invent the idea of the heel. But he perfected it. In 1941 he created the character "Gorgeous George." Gorgeous George was the first wrestler to use entrance music. He strutted into the ring in fancy robes and insisted on being perfumed by his servant before each match. George also cheated every chance he could, and he bragged about it.

Hulk Hogan became the heel "Hollywood Hogan" (left) in the mid-1990s. In the early 2000s, he turned back to the heroic character that had made him famous.

Hulk Hogan

At 6 feet, 8 inches (203 centimeters) tall, Terry Gene Bollea is one large guy. Wrestling promoter Vince McMahon Sr. gave him the nickname "Hulk Hogan." Hogan soon became the fans' favorite babyface. He played the role of the hardworking, all-American guy. Hogan remained the most popular pro wrestler for years. Most of his matches followed a normal pattern. Hogan fought fiercely at first. Then he would weaken and almost be defeated. That's when his fans would pump up the volume. Hogan seemed to feed off of the audience's support. He called it "hulking up." Finally, he would get a second wind and triumph.

FUN FACT:

Many pro wrestlers have been both babyfaces and heels. They change back and forth to keep fans interested.

SIGNATURE MOVES

A signature move is a move that a wrestler is known for. Other wrestlers may use the same move, but they often give it a slight twist and a different name. In fact, most moves have several names or variations. Check out a few of the most famous signature moves.

THE ELBOW DROP

A wrestler jumps onto his opponent. He lands with his elbow jabbing into his opponent.

Also called: The People's Elbow

Made famous by: Shawn Michaels, The Rock

THE POWERBOMB

The opponent is lifted up and slammed back-first onto the mat.

Also called: Jackknife, Tiger Driver

Made famous by: Vader and Kevin Nash

ACE CRUSHER

The wrestler reaches over his shoulder and wraps his arm around the opponent's neck. Then he falls down backward, slamming his opponent's face either into the mat or into his shoulder.

Also called: Diamond Cutter, Stone Cold Stunner

Made famous by: Johnny Ace, Diamond Dallas Page, and Stone Cold Steve Austin

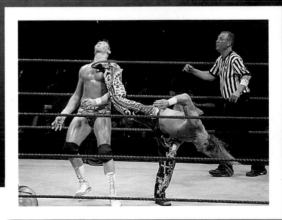

SUPERKICK

A wrestler delivers a karate-style kick to his opponent's head.

Also called: Sweet Chin Music

Made famous by: Chris Adams, Shawn Michaels, and Lance Storm

THE CHOKE

A wrestler gets behind his opponent and wraps one arm around the opponent's neck. He uses his other arm to keep his opponent's head from moving.

Also called: the Sleeper, the Rear Naked Choke

Made famous by: Roddy Piper, Samoa Joe

PILEDRIVER

The wrestler turns his opponent upside down and then falls into a sitting or kneeling position. The fall drives his opponent's head into the mat.

Also called:

Tombstone Piledriver

Made famous by:

Karl Gotch and Undertaker

THE MOONSAULT

A wrestler climbs onto the ropes.
He does a backflip, landing on
his opponent.

Also called: Lionsault,
Starship Pain

Made famous by: Chris Jericho,
Ultimo Dragon

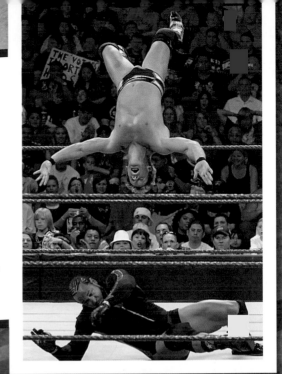

MADMAN FROM THE SUDAN

His real name is Larry Shreeve. But in
the ring he was known as "the Madman
from the Sudan" or "Abdullah the Butcher."
Shreeve started wrestling in the 1950s.
Today he is semi-retired. The Madman was
famous for his sneaky, aggressive style.
One of his signature moves was to pull out
a hidden fork and jab an opponent.

There have been thousands of pro wrestlers. But only a few have become household names.

Lou Thesz

Many consider Lou Thesz the greatest wrestler ever. He began his career in the 1930s. At 20 years old, Thesz became the youngest pro to wear a championship belt. Thesz's wrestling career spanned 40 years. At age 64, he became the oldest wrestler to win the championship.

Andre the Giant

Andre the Giant was 7 feet, 4 inches (224 cm) tall and weighed up to 500 pounds (227 kilograms). In the 1970s and 1980s, Andre was one of the best-known heels in wrestling. His fame led to movie roles. His best-known role was that of the lovable giant Fezzik in the movie *The Princess Bride*.

Ric Flair

Also known as "Nature Boy," Flair played a heel most of his career. He liked to taunt his opponents by saying, "To be the man, you gotta' beat the man." Like Gorgeous George, Flair dyed his hair blond and liked to strut around in fancy clothes.

Steve Austin

In the late 1990s, "Stone Cold" Steve Austin **feuded** constantly with WWE owner Vince McMahon Jr. Austin's rebellious image turned him into a wrestling superstar. He constantly bragged about how he could "whup" his opponents. In 2009 Austin was voted into the WWE Hall of Fame.

FUN FACT:

Former pro wrestler Jesse "The Body" Ventura went on to a successful political career. From 1999 to 2003, he served as governor of Minnesota.

feud—to have a long-running quarrel between two people or groups of people

Today's wrestling stars rule the ring. They often become stars in other areas such as music and movies too.

Chris Jericho

Chris Jericho has wrestled under many nicknames. They include "Lionheart" and the "Ayatollah of Rock 'n' Rolla." Jericho started as a babyface. But he has gone back and forth from babyface to heel many times. Jericho has won 22 WWE championships.

FUN FACT:

Chris Jericho is the lead singer of a heavy metal band and once hosted a TV game show.

John Cena

John Cena broke into pro wrestling in 2002. He quickly became a popular babyface. This rapping wrestler won the WWE World Championship nine times. Cena is also a singer in a hip-hop band and has starred in action movies.

WOMEN IN PRO WRESTLING

Women have been involved in pro wrestling from the beginning. But most of them have worked as valets to men. One of the earliest female wrestlers was Lillian Ellison. She began her career as a valet, but Ellison eventually stepped into the ring herself. When asked why she wrestled, Ellison said "for the moolah." This led to her nickname the Fabulous Moolah.
In 1956 Moolah became the Women's World Champion. She held the title for 30 years.

Women made few appearances in the ring again until the late 1990s. That is when Chyna became a WWE star. Today women's roles in wrestling are growing. Both WWE and TNA have women's divisions. Hundreds of women try out each year.

valet—a person who walks to the ring with a wrestler and helps the wrestler during matches

Famous Families

Some of today's most famous wrestlers have wrestling in their blood. Look at a wrestler's family tree, and you'll often find many more wrestlers.

Dwayne Johnson

Dwayne "The Rock" Johnson is one of the most famous wrestlers in the world. He is the son of "Soulman" Rocky Johnson. Dwayne is also the grandson of High Chief Peter Maivia, a **Samoan** wrestler known for his long hair and tattoos. After playing football in college, Dwayne had his father teach him about wrestling. He started his career as a babyface. But he soon changed his nickname to "The Rock" and became one of wrestling's superstar heels. Like John Cena, Dwayne Johnson has also starred in movies.

Samoan—a person from either Samoa or American Samoa

Bret "Hitman" Hart was a popular wrestler in the 1990s.

The Harts

Hall-of-fame wrestler Stu Hart began a wrestling **legacy**. He worked as a wrestler, a promoter, and a trainer. Hart began his wrestling career in the 1940s. He started a wrestling training school in his basement, where he taught his sons to wrestle. Several of his children joined the family business. His sons Bret and Owen gained great fame as WWE wrestlers.

legacy—something handed down
from one generation to another

A **gimmick** might be a flashy outfit or a crazy type of match-up. Often the wrestlers themselves are gimmicks. They can be incredibly tall or very short or just plain ugly. Sometimes a wrestler's personality or wrestling style serves as a gimmick. These personalities play a key role in the feuds that wrestlers pick with each other.

The Giant of the Ring

One of the tallest men in pro wrestling was Jorge "Giant" Gonzalez. He stood 7 feet, 6 inches (230 cm) tall—at least a head taller than most of his opponents. Gonzalez made his appearance more fearsome by wearing a hair-covered bodysuit with giant muscles painted on it.

gimmick—a clever trick or idea used to get people's attention

The Smallest Champion

On the other extreme is Dylan Postl, who wrestles under the name Hornswoggle. At 4 feet, 5 inches (135 cm) tall, he is one of the smallest pro wrestlers. In 2007 Hornswoggle became the smallest and youngest wrestler to ever win the WWE cruiserweight championship. He was 21 years old.

The French Angel

In the 1940s, a wrestler named Maurice Tillet became known as the French Angel. He suffered from a disease that left his face badly bloated. His frightening appearance drew large crowds.

FUN FACT:

Many wrestlers use masks as part of their gimmick. The first masked wrestler appeared in 1873 in Paris, France. His stage name was "The Masked Wrestler."

Nothing pleases a crowd of wrestling fans like a gimmick match. In these matches, many of the usual rules are called off.

Steel Cage Match

Wrestlers face off in a ring with barred walls and a roof. None of them are allowed to leave until one wrestler is pinned or gives up. Sometimes the cage's walls are electrified or surrounded by flames.

Casket Match

A casket is put near the ring. The goal is for one wrestler to get his opponent into the casket and close it.

Ladder Match

An object is placed high above the ring. Usually it is a championship belt. A ladder is also put in the ring. The winner is the first person to use the ladder to retrieve the object.

Tag Team Match

Two or more wrestlers work together as a team. Usually only one wrestler per team is allowed in the ring at a time. In order for them to change places, the partner in the ring must tag the teammate.

One of the best-known types of gimmicks is the feud. Two or more wrestlers hold a grudge against each other. They wrestle each other repeatedly over time. Audiences love the constant conflict. When fans tire of one feud, wrestlers quit the old feud and start another.

Mildred Burke

Mildred Burke vs. June Byers

This 1954 match is considered one of the greatest wrestling events of all-time. Burke was an aging former champion. Byers was the young up-and-coming champion. The women had been at odds for years. The match was set up so that the winner had to pin the opponent twice. After more than an hour, both women had pinned their opponent once. But Burke got injured and the match had to stop. Many people think the match should have ended as a tie. But Byers was given the victory.

John Cena vs. Chris Jericho

In 2005 John Cena joined the weekly WWE program *RAW*. This put him in competition with Chris Jericho. Jericho played the heel to feud with babyface Cena, the current WWE champion. Jericho lost the first match to Cena. The next night they met in a "You're Fired" match. Whoever lost the match could no longer wrestle on *RAW*. Jericho lost again, and *RAW's* general manager fired him. He had to be carried out of the ring by security. But Jericho's firing did not last long. He has since come back to win the championship.

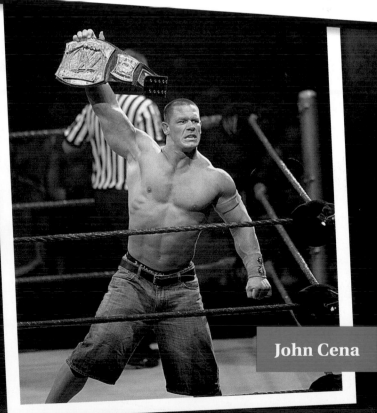

John Cena

Most wrestling fans tune into weekly programs like *RAW* and *Smackdown*. But the most anticipated wrestling event each year is WrestleMania. Check out a few of WrestleMania's most memorable moments.

Andre the Giant (left) and Hulk Hogan (right)

WrestleMania 3, 1987

Hulk Hogan squared off against Andre the Giant in front of 93,000 screaming fans at Michigan's Silverdome. Andre had Hogan on the ropes for most of the match. But Hogan managed to slam Andre and finish him off with a leg drop.

WrestleMania 17, 2001

Undertaker knocked out the referee in this match against Triple H. That allowed the rivals to fight dirty, which included some serious pounding with metal chairs. Undertaker took a lot of punishment from Triple H, but he still came out on top.

WrestleMania 23, 2007

At WrestleMania 23, Donald Trump and WWE owner Vince McMahon Jr. squared off in a "Battle of the Billionaires." Trump and McMahon had two wrestlers grapple in their places. McMahon's wrestler lost. As promised, McMahon shaved his head in front of more than 80,000 fans.

Donald Trump

Pro wrestling has grown incredibly since its humble carnival beginnings. Today thousands of fans pack arenas for shows like WrestleMania. The future of this popular entertainment form looks bright and action-packed.

GLOSSARY

chokehold (CHOHK-hohld)—a hold in which a wrestler wraps the arms or legs around an opponent's neck to cut off the air supply

feud (FYOOD)—to have a long-running quarrel between two people or groups of people

gimmick (GIM-ik)—a clever trick or idea used to get people's attention

legacy (LEG-uh-see)—something handed down from one generation to another

Samoan (suh-MOH-uhn)—a person from the Pacific islands of Samoa or American Samoa

signature move (SIG-nuh-chur MOOV)—the move for which a wrestler is best known; this move also is called a finishing move

valet (vah-LAY)—a person who walks to the ring with a wrestler and helps the wrestler during matches

READ MORE

Kaelberer, Angie Peterson. *The Fabulous, Freaky, Unusual History of Pro Wrestling.* Unusual Histories. Mankato, Minn.: Capstone Press, 2011.

O'Shei, Tim. *John Cena.* Stars of Pro Wrestling. Mankato, Minn.: Capstone Press, 2010.

Shields, Brian. *CM Punk.* DK Readers. London; New York: DK Pub., 2009.

INTERNET SITES

FactHound offers a safe, fun way to find Internet sites related to this book. All of the sites on FactHound have been researched by our staff.

Here's all you do:

Visit *www.facthound.com*

Type in this code: 9781429660082

Super-cool stuff! Check out projects, games and lots more at **www.capstonekids.com**

INDEX